WRITING ACTIVITIES SAMPLER
from Evan-Moor

Y0-EKT-898

Enjoy using these activities from Evan-Moor writing titles. We hope that they will enrich your instructional program, show you how effective and easy-to-use our materials are, and encourage you to try some of the many writing titles for grades K–6 published by Evan-Moor.

▼ ▼ ▼ ▼ The Activities ▼ ▼ ▼ ▼

Note: Each activity displays the grade level desigation of the book from which it is taken. Many activities, however, may be appropriate for a wider grade span.

▲ ▲ ▲ ▲ ▲ ▲ ▲ ▲ ▲ ▲ ▲ ▲ ▲ ▲

A Friendly Letter
Basic Form

Name _____

your address

number street

city, state zip code

month day, year

date

greeting

body of letter

Dear _____ ,

indent

Your Friend,   closing

signature

_____

Draw a caterpillar.

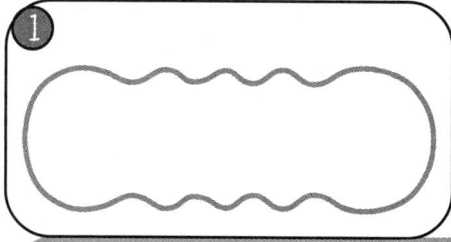

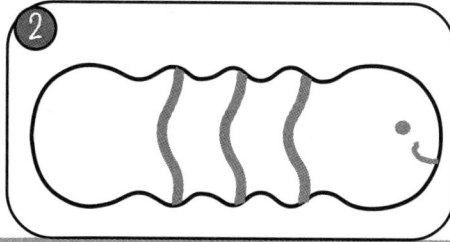

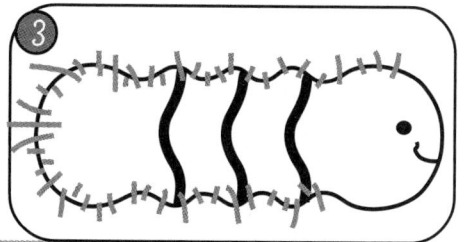

1

2

3

Write about the caterpillar.

Who or what?   _____

Did what?   _____

Where?   _____

When?   _____

Why?   _____

Write a sentence.

_____

_____

Truck

Prewriting Activities

Read

The Little Black Truck by Libba Moore Gray; Simon & Schuster, 1994.

Truck Trouble by Angela Toyston; DK Merchandise, 1998.

Trucks by Byron Barton; HarperCollins Juvenile Books, 1998.

Trucks by Gail Gibbons; HarperCollins Publishers, 1985.

My Trucks by Kirsten Hall; Children's Press, 1995.

Big Rigs by John Malam; Simon & Schuster, 1998.

Truck Song by Diane Siebert; HarperTrophy, 1987.

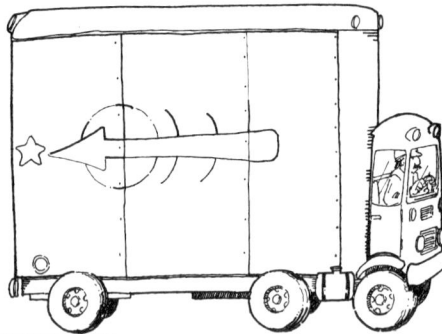

Get Ready to Write

1. Share a book about trucks with students. Discuss the different types of trucks. Ask students to name them and explain how they are used.

2. Bring in a variety of toy trucks and ask students to bring in toy trucks they have. Review the names of the various trucks and their functions. Put the toy trucks into categories by size, color, or function.

Writing Activities

Individual Books

- **Draw a Story**
  Reproduce the cover and several blank pages. Help students think of their own topics for stories or use one of the following ideas:

  Trucks
  Students are to draw one kind of truck on each page.

  Colorful Trucks
  Students are to draw a different colored truck on each page. Have them write the color of the truck at the bottom of each page.

- **Complete the Sentences**
  Reproduce the cover, a blank form, and the cloze form. Students complete the sentences to create a story, and then draw a picture on the blank form.

- **Write a Story**
  Reproduce the cover and several lined forms. Students write their own truck stories. Possible story starters:

All Aboard the Fire Truck	*Fun with Toy Trucks*
Gus, the Garbage Truck	*Farmer Fred's Pickup Truck*
If I Had a Truck, It Would Be...	*Red Truck, Blue Truck, Old Truck, New Truck*

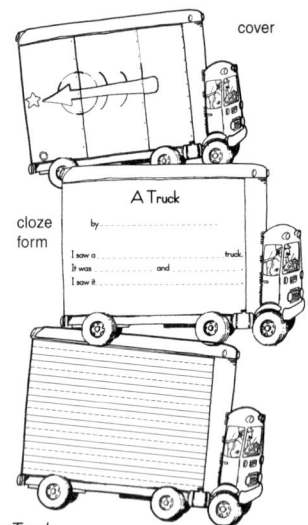

cover

cloze form

A Truck

lined form for written stories

Group Books

- **Where's the Truck?—Positional Words**
  Each student will need a blank truck form and a truck from page 132. Brainstorm and list places the truck might be located (over the bridge, around the corner, up the hill, under a tree, on the truck scales, etc.). Students will color, cut out, and paste the truck to the blank form. They then draw the background to show where the truck is located and write a sentence describing the location of the truck. (*The garbage truck is in front of the house. My yellow fire truck is racing over the bridge.*) Compile student pages and attach a cover.

- **Trucks at Work**
  Each student will need one or more lined forms. Ask students to write fiction or nonfiction stories about a truck and the work it does. Compile student pages and attach a cover.

The fire truck went down the street.

clip art

Note: Reproduce this book cover for each student.

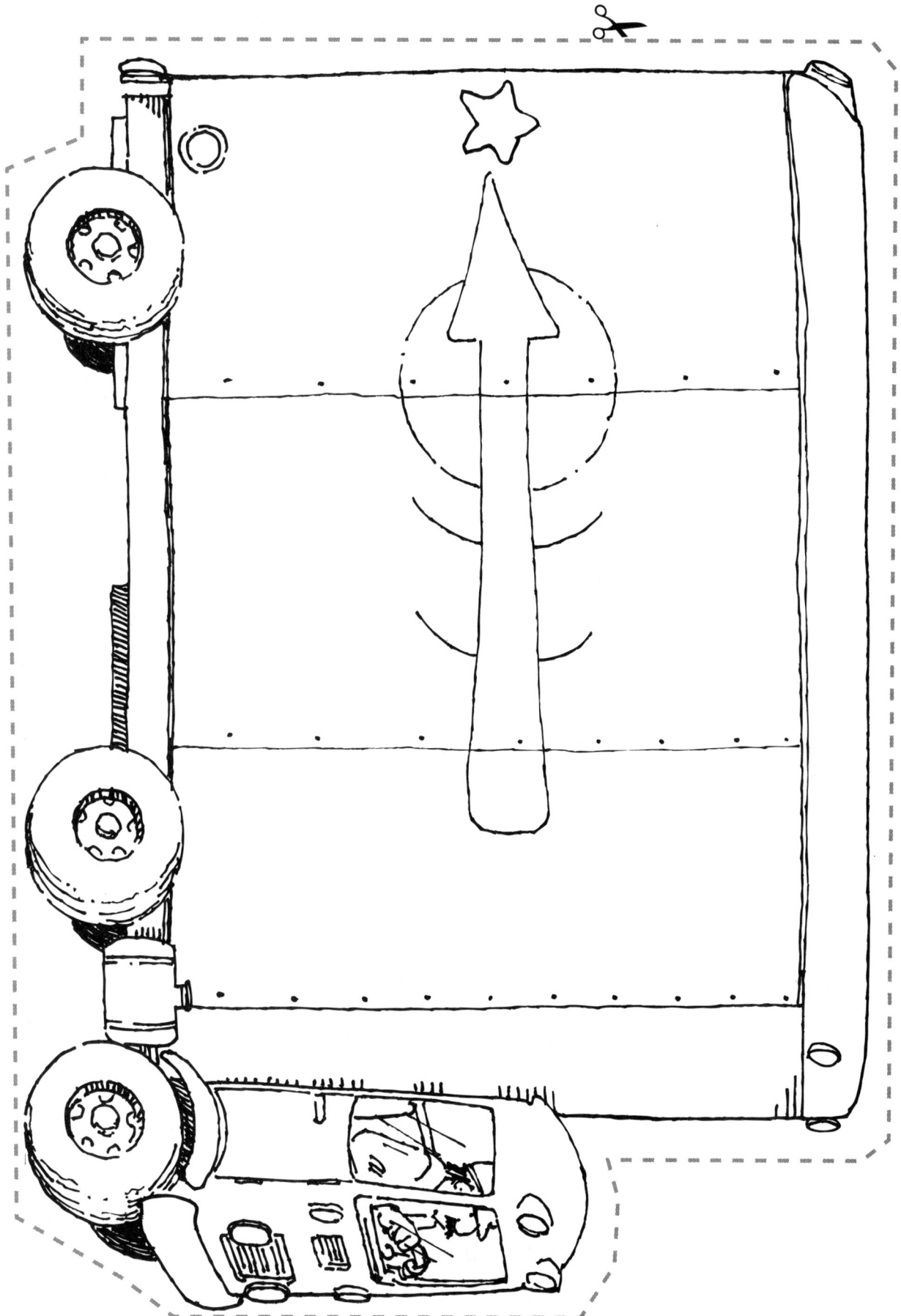

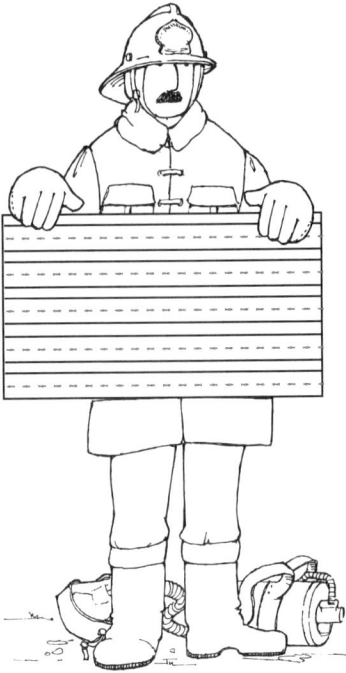

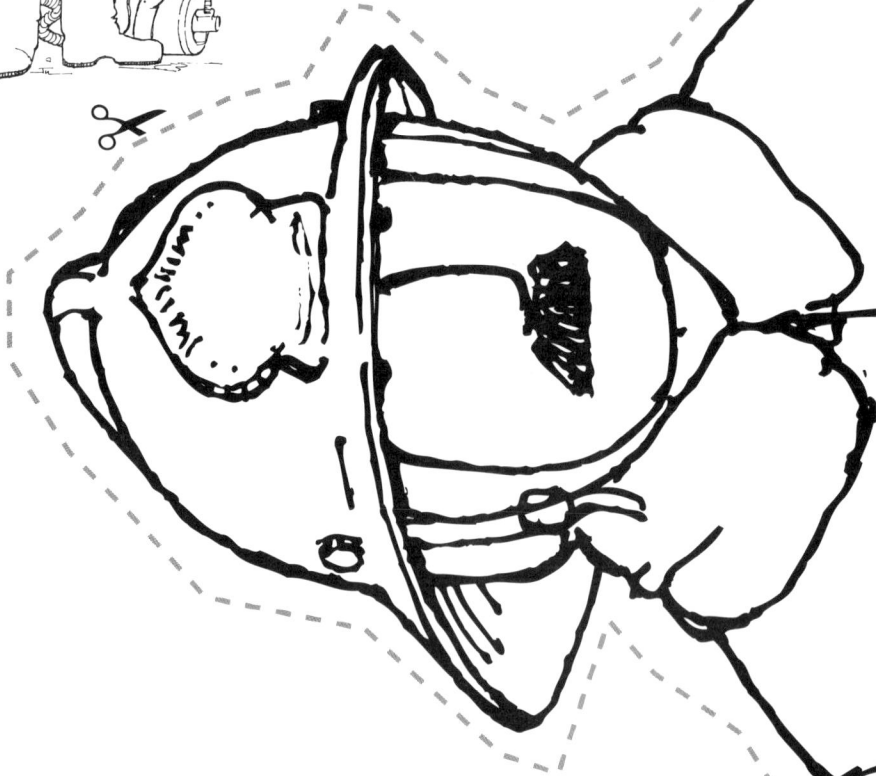

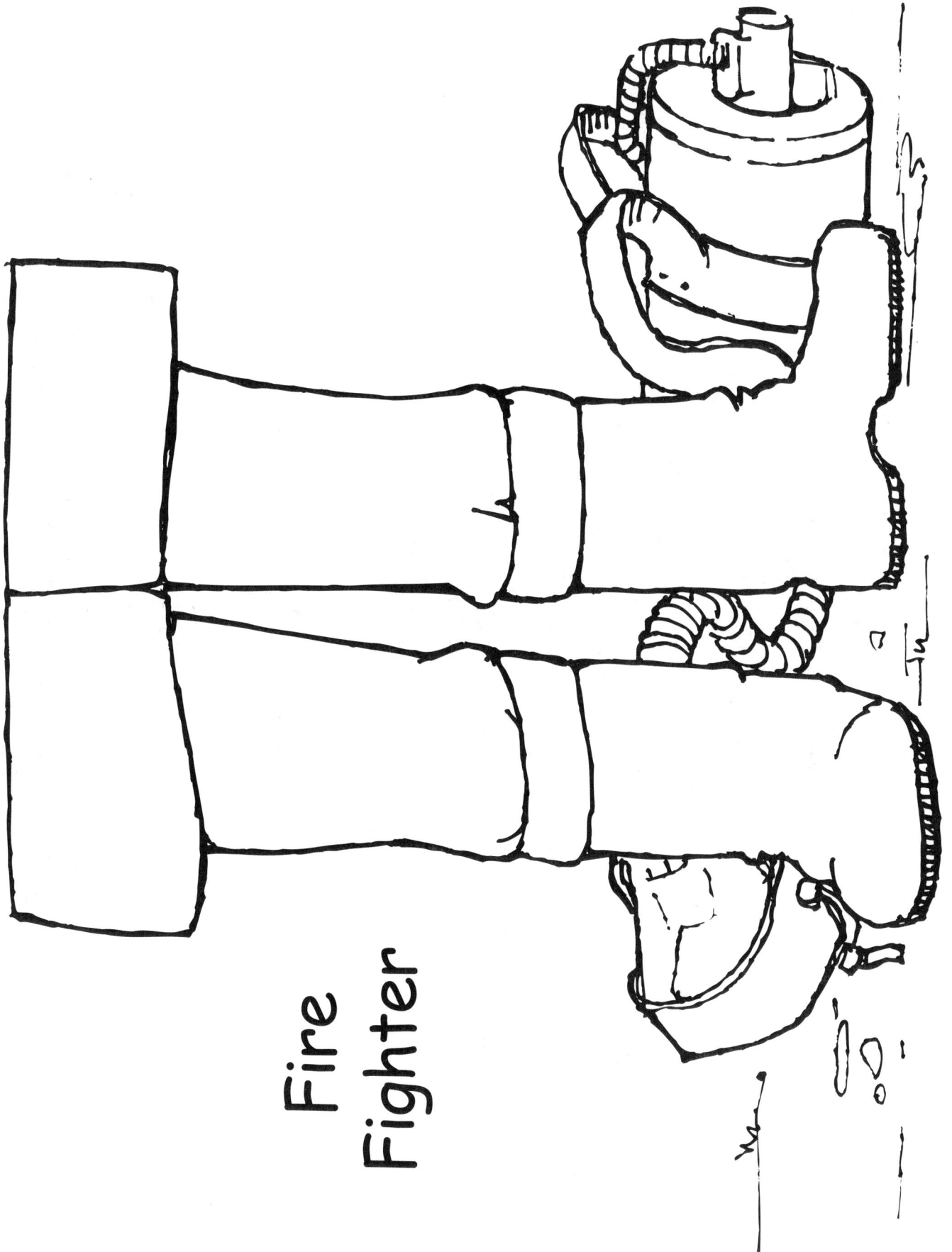

Fire
Fighter

How to Draw a Cat

1

2

3

4

Follow the Steps to Draw

Name _____

From *Draw…Then Write, Grades 4–6* (EMC 773)
©2001 by Evan-Moor Corp. See pages 16-17 for more information.

The spaceship landed.

1. **Brainstorm**
   Fill in one category at a time, beginning with describing words. List children's suggestions on the chalkboard or on a chart.

2. **Oral Sentences**
   Allow time for children to create many oral sentences using the words and phrases written on the chalkboard.

3. **Write**
   Have the children follow the same steps to complete the written activity on the following page.

4. **Proof and Correct**

	describing (adjective)	who or what? (noun)	did what? (verb)	where?	when?
The		spaceship	landed		

Add these words and phrases to increase vocabulary and develop new concepts.

describing words:
1. metallic
2. swift
3. graceful
4. foreign

who or what?
1. vehicle
2. transport
3. shuttlecraft

did what?
1. approached
2. circled
3. escaped
4. ejected the equipment
5. encountered unusual life-forms

where?
1. a distant planet
2. around several asteroids
3. from gravity's pull
4. from inside the ship
5. throughout the universe

when?
1. after a long journey
2. before landing
3. just in time
4. after take off
5. during its explorations

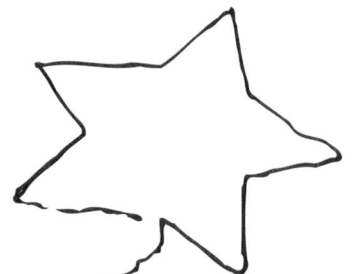

The Spaceship

_____

name

_____

date

How many sentences can you write?

_____

_____

_____

_____

_____

_____

_____

_____

_____

_____

_____

_____

_____

_____

_____

_____

_____

_____

_____

Illustrate one sentence on the back of this paper.

From _Write a Super Sentence, Grades 1–3_ (EMC 205)
©1997 by Evan-Moor Corp. See pages 16-17 for more information.

Fish Kite

Prewriting

Literature Connections
A Carp for Kimiko by Virginia L. Kroll; Charlesbridge Publishing, 1993.
Chibi: A True Story from Japan by Barbara Brenner and Julia Takaya; Clarion Books, 1996.
Colors of Japan by Holly Littlefield; Carolrhoda Books, Inc., 1997.
Lucky Song by Vera B. Williams; Greenwillow, 1997.
Moonlight Kite by Helen E. Buckley; Lothrop, Lee & Shepard Books, 1997.
A Sky Full of Kites by Osmond Molarsky; Tricycle Press, 1996.

Concrete Experiences
After reading a nonfiction account of the Japanese tradition of flying fish kites to celebrate their children, have your students make fish kites to fly by your classroom entrance on Children's Day, May 5.

Let the Writing Begin

Emergent Writers

- **Feast of Flags**
  Students draw a long pole with a fish kite for each child in their family. They may label the kites with family members' names.

- **Flying in the Wind**
  Students draw things that fly in the wind and tell about their drawings.

Beginning Writers

- **Kodomo-No-Hi (Children's Day)**
  Students draw a pole with fish kites. Then they copy and complete the sentence.

  On Children's Day, fish kites are flown to _____.

- **Celebrate**
  Students draw a celebration they observe. Then they copy and complete the sentence.

  At my house we always celebrate _____.

Independent Writers

- **Strong and Persistent**
  Fish kites are made in the shape of carp. Carp are strong fish that swim up fast-moving streams. To the Japanese they symbolize courage. Have students write to tell how these fish demonstrate strength and persistence.

- **The Magic Kite**
  Students write a tale about a kite with magical powers.

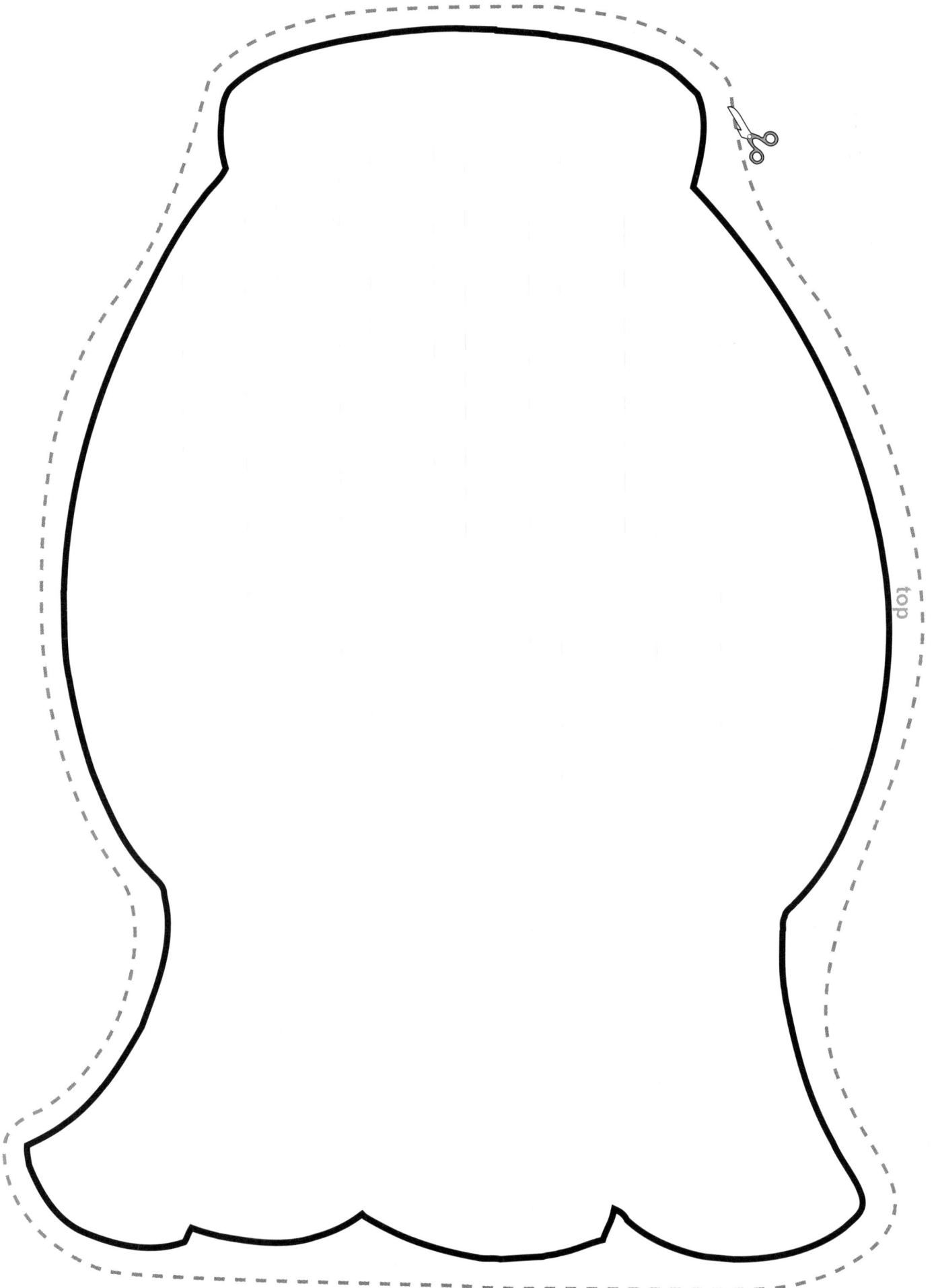

top

Name:

The First and Sixteenth Presidents

Although George Washington and Abraham Lincoln were both presidents of the United States, their lives were very different.

I think the biggest difference was

Write two or more supporting sentences.

Although George Washington and Abraham Lincoln lived at different times, their lives were similar in many ways.

Essential Writing Skills

Evan-Moor
EDUCATIONAL PUBLISHERS

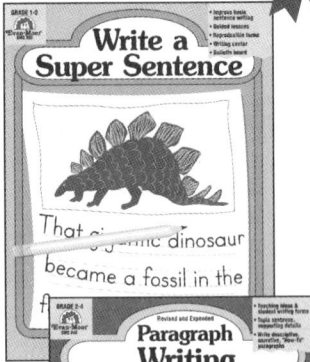

BEST SELLER

Write a Super Sentence *
Grades 1–3
Step-by-step guided lessons. Students brainstorm adjectives, nouns, verbs, and where-and-when phrases, then use them to expand a simple sentence. Includes 15 lessons, teaching ideas, reproducible forms, writing center, and bulletin board.
64 pp. $8.99   EMC 205

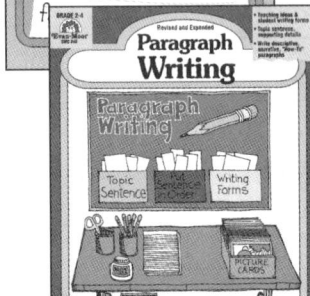

Paragraph Writing *
Grades 2–4
Teach beginning paragraph writing skills. Includes teaching ideas, reproducible forms, and center with ready-to-use materials. Topics: parts of a paragraph, types of paragraphs, and planning paragraphs.
80 pp. $9.99   EMC 246

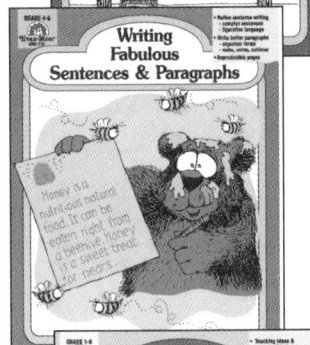

Writing Fabulous Sentences & Paragraphs *
Grades 4–6
Improve and refine sentence and paragraph skills. Lessons and activities progress from writing sentences to writing paragraphs. There are complete teacher instructions and over 70 reproducible models and student writing forms. Answer key is provided.
112 pp. $10.99   EMC 575

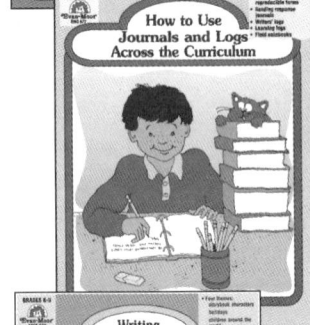

How to Use Journals and Logs Across the Curriculum
Grades 1–6
Step-by-step teacher information and reproducible forms, 5 types of logs and journals (reading response journals, writers' logs, learning logs, dialogue journals, field notebooks). How to get started and how to evaluate.
64 pp. $8.99   EMC 577

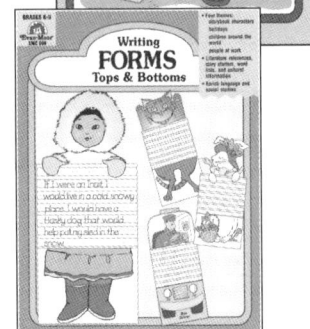

Writing Forms— Tops & Bottoms
Grades K–3
Students will be motivated to do their best work when you showcase their reports, stories, or handwriting with these two-piece forms. Students color and cut out; you put their papers in the middle.
160 pp. $16.99   EMC 596

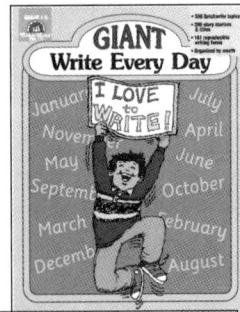

Giant Write Every Day
Grades 1–6
The MOST COMPREHENSIVE writing resource a teacher can own! 300 "Quickwrites"—25 topics each month for short, daily practice; 209 story starters and titles for longer, more formal writings; 151 reproducible writing forms. 12 monthly sections.
176 pp. $19.99   EMC 775

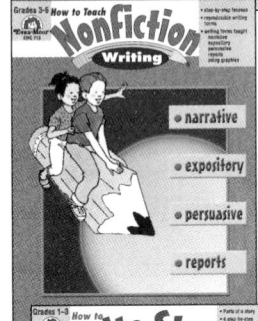

How to Teach Nonfiction Writing *
Grades 3–6
Teacher directions and reproducible writing forms guide the development of the following writing types: narrative, expository, persuasive, research reports, using graphic components, and more. Reproducible charts describe the characteristics of each type of writing and give steps to follow.
96 pp. $12.99   EMC 719

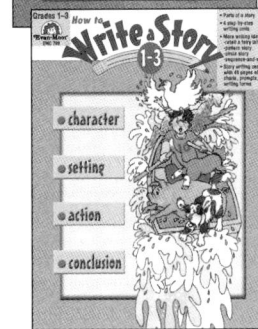

How to Write a Story *
Grades 1–3
Four step-by-step writing units help young writers create sensible stories with a beginning, a middle, and an end. Includes a story-writing center with reproducible charts, prompts, and writing forms.
96 pp. $12.99   EMC 799

How to Write a Story *
Grades 4–6
Lessons and reproducibles to help students learn the parts of a story, reproducible planning forms, and guidelines for writing in six different genres. Includes a story-writing center with reproducible charts, prompts, and writing forms.
96 pp. $12.99   EMC 794

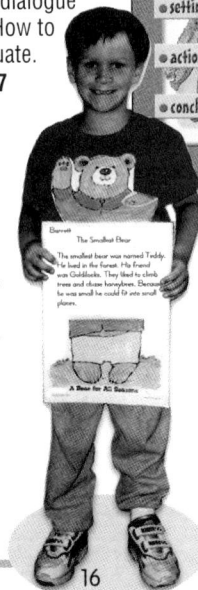

Correlated to State * Standards

Essential Writing Skills

Evan-Moor EDUCATIONAL PUBLISHERS

- ## Expository writing
- ## Narrative writing
- ## Creative writing
- ## Poetry writing

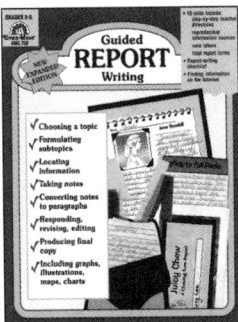

Guided Report Writing *
Grades 3–6
Following an 8-step process, students learn to locate information and synthesize it into an organized report. You get everything you need to guide your students in writing 10 reports. Each lesson includes step-by-step teacher directions, reproducible information sources, graphic components, a note taker, and a final report form.
96 pp. $12.99   EMC 732

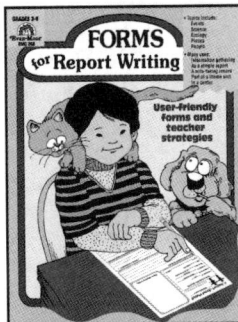

Forms for Report Writing
Grades 3–6
Simple forms for gathering and organizing factual information. Five topics: events, science, ecology, places, people.
64 pp. $8.99   EMC 288

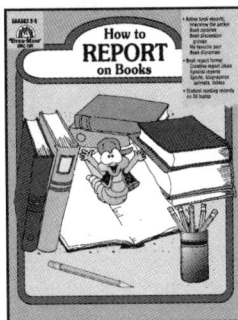

How to Report on Books
Grades 2–5
A variety of interesting ways to report on books—create a new cover for a book, "sell" a book to classmates, make a video book review, make puppets of a book's main characters, role-play an interview with the author, or assemble a book diorama. There are also a number of traditional written book report forms, each emphasizing different aspects of a book.
80 pp. $10.99   EMC 299

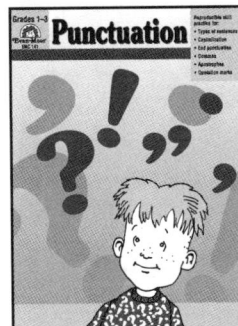

Punctuation
Grades 1–3
Reproducible skill practice for sentence types, capitalization, and punctuation. Covers all the major primary-level skills. Progressive difficulty allows you to meet individual needs.
80 pp. $9.99   EMC 141

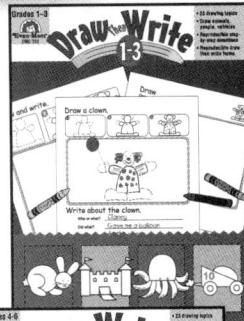

Draw...Then Write
Grades 1–3
Newly revised and expanded! Students follow step-by-step drawing lessons and write about the completed pictures. Writing exercises take students from simple to more complex writing tasks.
96 pp. $12.99   EMC 731

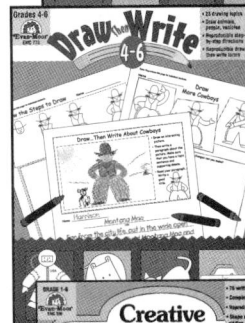

Draw...Then Write
Grades 4–6
Students follow picture directions to draw animals, people, and vehicles. They then write a paragraph about what they have drawn.
96 pp. $12.99   EMC 773

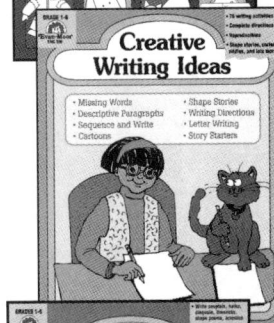

Creative Writing Ideas
Grades 1–6
A variety of motivating lessons. 11 types of writing experiences are presented, including draw and write, riddles, sequence and write, and letter writing. Projects are accompanied by reproducible writing forms.
96 pp. $12.99   EMC 206

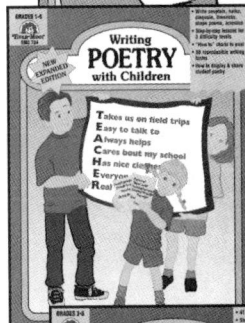

Writing Poetry with Children
Grades 1–6
A step-by-step guide for teaching students to write couplets, cinquain, haiku, and limericks. You get everything you need, including reproducible instructions and illustrated writing forms. We even provide a bibliography of poetry books, a list of poetry terms, and ideas for sharing poetry.
96 pp. $12.99   EMC 734

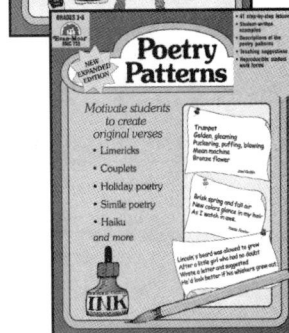

Poetry Patterns
Grades 3–6
You get over 40 lessons in writing poetry. Includes couplets, metaphor poetry, haiku, limericks, onomatopoeia, and recipe poetry! You also get a variety of ways to share poetry: display boards, charts, banners, newsletters, and books. Student-written samples included for each lesson.
96 pp. $12.99   EMC 733

* Correlated to State Standards

At the Pond

Fill in the bubbles.

From *Creative Writing Ideas, Grades 1–6* (EMC 206)
©1997 by Evan-Moor Corp. See pages 16-17 for more information.

Note: Students write daily for five to ten minutes. Be sure to conduct prewriting activities—discuss words, ideas, and experiences related to the topic.

January
Quickwrite Topics

My New Year's Resolutions	**A Bad Cold**	**In My Pocket**	**Elephants**	**If I had a camera, I would...**
Before I go to school, I...	**Waffles**	**Green Things**	**Birthday Cake**	**My Nickname**
A Bear in Winter	**When my relatives come...**	**A Mouse in My House**	**Thunder and Lightning**	**Balloons**
Sounds That Make Me Happy	**Teeth**	**The Best Taste in the World**	**If I found $5...**	**List as many "p" words as you can**
I am curious when...	**Liver**	**Why Zebras Have Stripes**	**I lost my...**	**Trees**

From *Giant Write Every Day, Grades 1–6* (EMC 775)
©1997 by Evan-Moor Corp. See pages 16-17 for more information.

Popping

Imagine that you are a kernel of popcorn. You have just been dumped into a large container. You hear a voice say, "Plug it in. It's ready to pop." Describe what happens as you are popped. Be sure to include things that you see and hear and smell and feel.

How Did You Get to Know the Character?

Your Name	Character's Name

Pages	What the character says	What I think about this

Pages	What the character thinks	What I think about this

Pages	What the character does	What I think about this

Pages	What other characters say	What I think about this

Pages	What the storyteller says	What I think about this

The Shoe
A Shape Book

Materials

Class book:
- shoe pattern on page 36
- 2 sheets of 9" x 12" (23 x 30.5 cm) construction paper or tagboard
- a brightly colored shoelace
- student writing paper
- hole punch, scissors
- glue, felt pens

Individual book:
Reproduce the pattern on page 36 for each student to color, cut, and use as a cover for an original story. Use roving or yarn to lace the book.

1 Color and cut out the pattern.

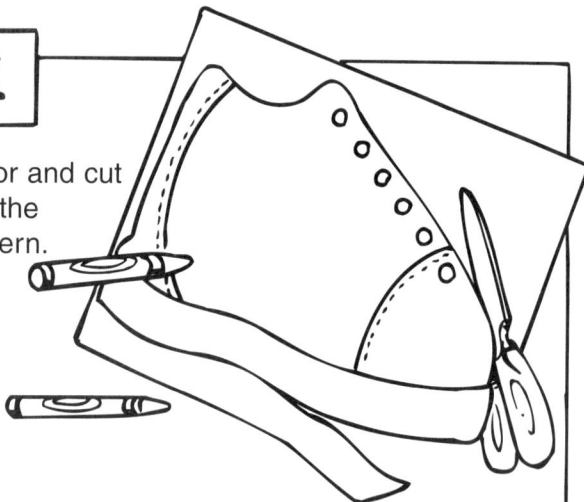

2 Glue the pattern to the construction paper. Cut around the shape, leaving a small border. This is the front cover.

Cut the back cover and student writing papers in the same shape.

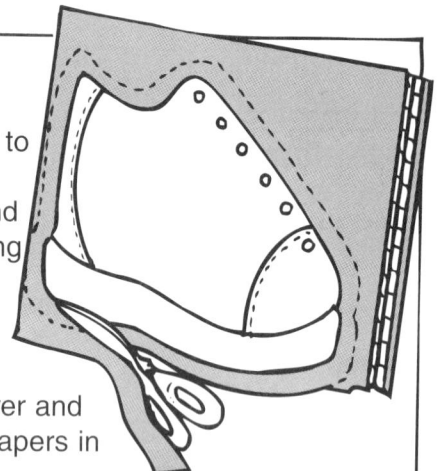

3 Staple the writing papers to the back cover.

4 Assemble all layers. Punch holes along the top.

Lace the shoelace through the holes.

From *Literature and Writing Connections, Grades 1–6* (EMC 777)
©1997 by Evan-Moor Corp. See inside front cover for more information.

Writing Connections

Don't Walk Through That Mud!

Write a story from a sneaker's point of view.

Magic Sneakers

Where did you find them? What can they do for you? What happened when you wore them?

How Sneakers Got Their Name

Write a story to tell how you think sneakers earned their name.

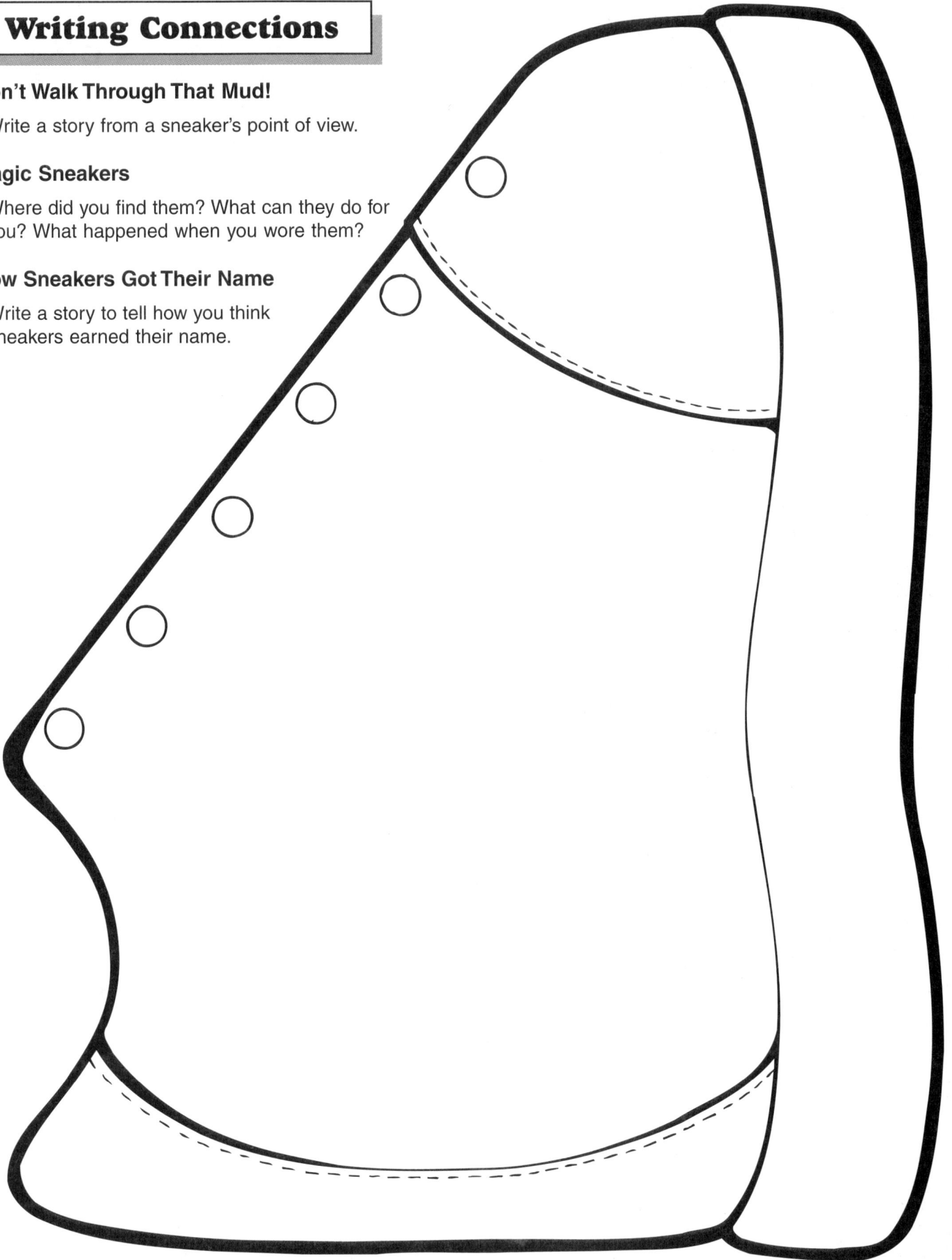

A Pattern Story

A Simple Group Story

Read a pattern book such as *Fortunately* by Remy Charlip (Aladdin Paperbacks, 1993) or *That's Good! That's Bad!* by Margery Cuyler (Owlet, 1993).

Tell students that they are going to write a group pattern story. Follow these steps:

• Brainstorm to create a list of good things that could happen. Write a bad thing that could follow each good thing.

good: We're going to Grandma's.

bad: I get carsick.

good: I get to sit in the front seat.

good: My cousin gave me his bike.

bad: The bike has a flat tire.

good: My dad fixed it.

page 25

• Using the form on page 25, students each write one "Good, Bad, Good" page.

• Bind the completed pages into a cover for a class book.

Name _____

Good, Bad, Good

The good thing is _____

The bad thing is _____

The good thing is _____

A Pattern Story   How to Write a Story • EMC 799 • ©2001 by Evan-Moor Corp. 25

Name _____

Good, Bad, Good

The good thing is _____

_____

_____

_____

_____

The bad thing is _____

_____

_____

_____

_____

The good thing is _____

_____

_____

_____

_____

Question Poetry

Question poetry asks questions about the subject. There are usually four questions.
The pattern is AABB.

Do trees get tired of standing around all day?
Do they wish they could go out and play?
Do they get tired of birds nesting in their hair?
Do they wish they could sit in a very comfortable chair?
Kevin Mullins

Do trees get tired of standing around all day?

Imagine that the subject is alive.

Do they wish they could go out and play?
Do they get tired of birds nesting in their hair?

Ask sensitive questions.

Do they wish they could sit in a very comfortable chair?

End with a question that sounds as if you are finished.

Suggestions

The subject of a question poem can be anything (building, car, plant, animal, etc.) or anyone (friend, parent, hero, character in a book, etc.). The challenge for students is to come up with four questions that give personality to the subject. Encourage students to try to change moods as they write, to add interest to the poem.

From *Poetry Patterns, Grades 3–6* (EMC 733)
©1999 by Evan-Moor Corp. See pages 16-17 for more information.

Name _____

> **Question** poetry asks questions about something or someone.
> There are usually four questions. The pattern is AABB.

1 Decide on a subject. Think of the kinds of questions you would ask about that person or object.

Question 1:

_____

Question 2:

_____

Question 3:

_____

Question 4:

_____

2 Adjust your wording to fit the rhyming pattern.

Copy and illustrate your poem here.

-- -- -- -- -- -- -- -- -- -- -- -- -- -- -- -- -- --

_____
title

by _____

_____

_____

_____

_____

Describe the Characters

Underline the words and phrases that describe the zookeeper.

Circle the words and phrases that describe the monkey.

Make an **X** on the words and phrases that describe the elephant.

You will not use all of the phrases.

enormous	chatters noisily	wearing work clothes
whisks flies with her tail	sings as he works	stands large and tall
wet from head to foot	little brown monkey	big ears flap back and forth
hanging by his hand	feeding the elephant	surprised guy
agile trunk	watches the animals	holding onto a piece of fruit
squirts the zookeeper	wrinkled skin	working hard
trumpets to her calf	swinging up and down	standing on four big feet

Select one character. Using the descriptive words and phrases you marked, write a paragraph to introduce that character to your reader.

_____

_____

_____

_____

_____

Name _____

Describe the Setting

Underline the phrases below that describe this setting.

long grass waving in the wind	cool breezes	dark shadows
giant cactus	coiled snake	robins hunting worms
heat shimmering above the land	high noon	rolling sand dunes
elf owls hiding in holes	hot and dry	pools of cool water
grains of golden sand	elephant eating leaves	hot winds blowing
icy snowflakes falling from the sky	night coming soon	strange night noises

Using the underlined phrases, write a paragraph describing the setting to your readers.

_____

_____

_____

_____

Report on a Current Event

Look in the newspaper. Choose an event that interests you.

OUR TIMES

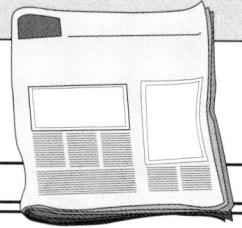

DATE: _____   Volume 1

Paste a headline here or create your own.

Event: _____
_____

Name the people involved in this event and their involvement.

_____
_____
_____
_____
_____

Briefly describe the main points of this event.

_____
_____
_____
_____
_____
_____
_____

List four reasons why this event is important.

_____
_____
_____
_____

What are some probable outcomes of the event?

_____
_____
_____
_____

Name _____

I Vote for Computers

Computers are important to my future because _____

_____

_____

_____

_____

I know that they will help _____

_____

_____

_____

_____

I am glad that I can use computers.

Write More About It

Choose something that you think is important.
Try to convince your readers that they should recognize the importance.

From *Writing Fabulous Sentences & Paragraphs, Grades 4–6* (EMC 575)
©1997 by Evan-Moor Corp. See pages 16-17 for more information.

Name _____

Using Similes

A simile makes a comparison by using the words **like** or **as**.

I'm as gentle as a kitten.

Underline the similes in the description below.

My garden was quiet under its blanket of snow. The cornstalks stood like silent sentinels. No footprints crossed the untouched whiteness. Frost decorated the fence like a lacy curtain. Winter had come, like a quiet lullaby that lulled Autumn to sleep.

List some things that you could compare to the following items.

thunder	spinach	having a tooth filled

Write a simile using each word.

1. _____

2. _____

3. _____